Theory Paper   Grade 3   2019   A

Duration 1½ hours

TOTAL MARKS
100

Candidates should answer ALL questions.
Write your answers on this paper – no others will be accepted.
Answers must be written clearly and neatly – otherwise marks may be lost.

1   Add the time signature to each of these five melodies.

10

2   Add the correct rest(s) at the places marked ∗ in these two melodies to make each bar complete.

10

3 Name the key of each of the following scales. Where the key is minor, state whether the scale is in the harmonic or melodic form.

10

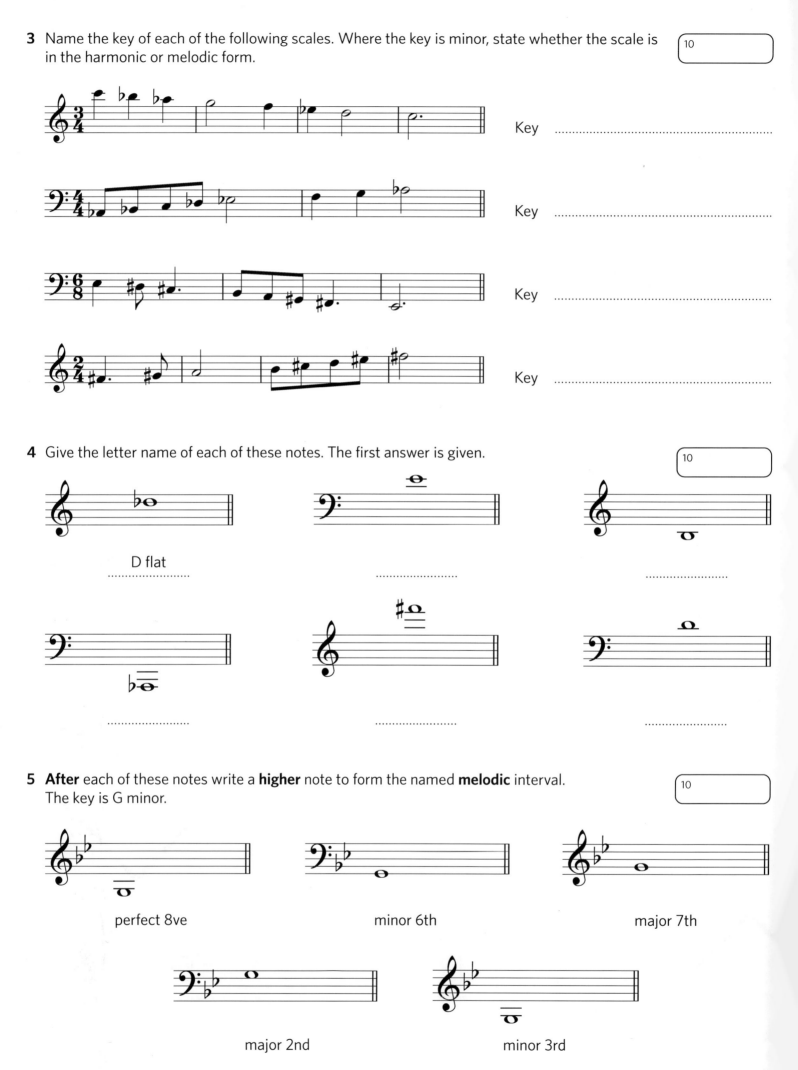

Key ....

Key ....

Key ....

Key ....

4 Give the letter name of each of these notes. The first answer is given.

10

D flat
....

....

....

....

....

....

5 **After** each of these notes write a **higher** note to form the named **melodic** interval. The key is G minor.

10

perfect 8ve

minor 6th

major 7th

major 2nd

minor 3rd

4

6 Add the correct clef and key signature to each of these tonic triads.

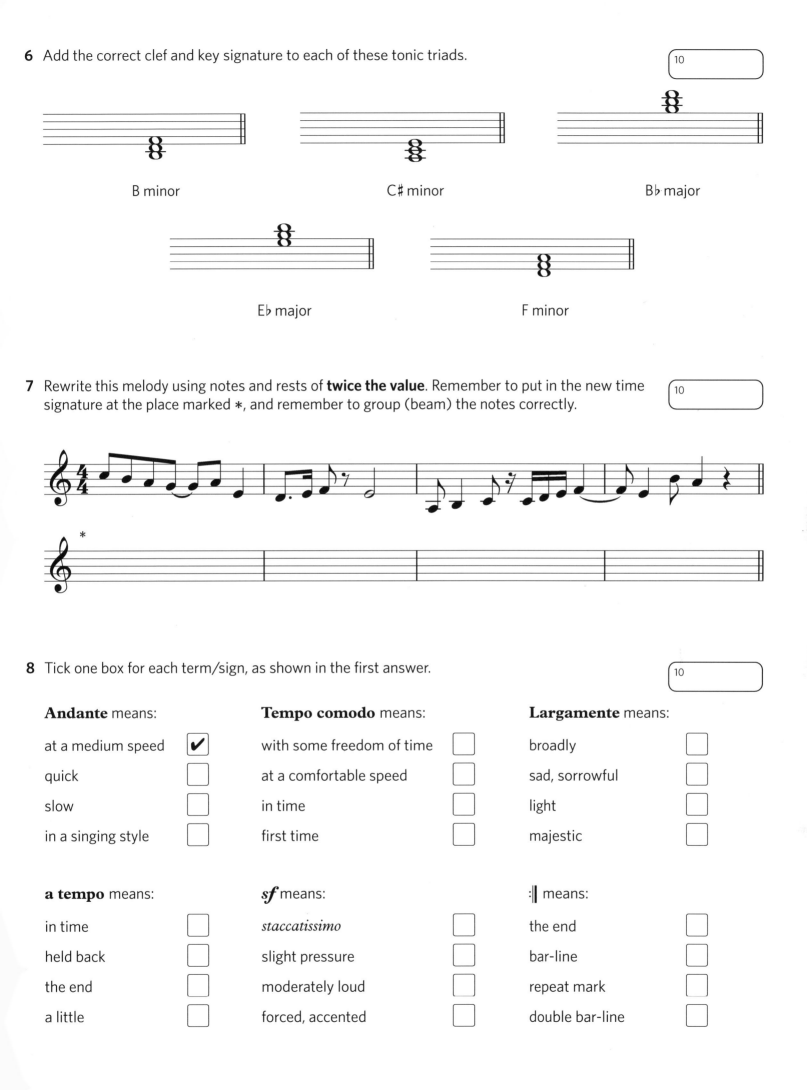

B minor C♯ minor B♭ major

E♭ major F minor

7 Rewrite this melody using notes and rests of **twice the value**. Remember to put in the new time signature at the place marked ∗, and remember to group (beam) the notes correctly.

8 Tick one box for each term/sign, as shown in the first answer.

Andante means:

at a medium speed ✔
quick ☐
slow ☐
in a singing style ☐

Tempo comodo means:

with some freedom of time ☐
at a comfortable speed ☐
in time ☐
first time ☐

Largamente means:

broadly ☐
sad, sorrowful ☐
light ☐
majestic ☐

a tempo means:

in time ☐
held back ☐
the end ☐
a little ☐

sf means:

staccatissimo ☐
slight pressure ☐
moderately loud ☐
forced, accented ☐

:‖ means:

the end ☐
bar-line ☐
repeat mark ☐
double bar-line ☐

5

9 Look at this melody and then answer the questions below.

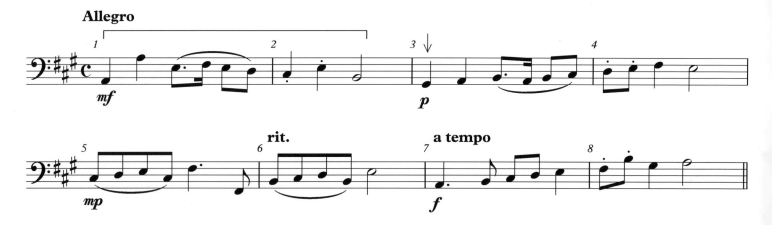

Write your answer to question (b) on the stave below.

(a) (i)   The melody is in the key of A major. Name the degree
            of the scale (e.g. 2nd, 3rd) of the first note of bar 3 (marked ↓).   ....

⌐10⌐

   (ii)   Which other key has the same key signature as A major?   ....

   (iii)   Describe the time signature as: simple or compound   ....

                                            duple, triple or quadruple   ....

   (iv)   Answer TRUE or FALSE to this sentence:

           The melody is to be played at the same speed throughout.   ....

   (v)   The first phrase has been marked with a bracket (⌐———⌐).
           Mark all the other phrases in the same way.

(b) Using the blank stave above question (a), write out the melody from the beginning of bar 5
     to the end of the music **an octave higher**, using the treble clef as shown.

⌐10⌐

Theory Paper   Grade 3   2019   B

Duration 1½ hours

TOTAL MARKS
100

Candidates should answer ALL questions.
Write your answers on this paper – no others will be accepted.
Answers must be written clearly and neatly – otherwise marks may be lost.

1   Add the missing bar-lines to each of these **three** melodies, which all begin on the first beat
of the bar.

10

2   Rewrite this melody with the notes correctly grouped (beamed).

10

3 **(a)** Add the correct clef and any necessary accidentals to make the scale of F♯ **melodic** minor. Do **not** use a key signature.

10

(b) Using semibreves (whole notes), write one octave of the scale of E♭ major, **ascending**, with key signature.

4 Name the key of each of these tonic triads.

10

....

....

5 Rewrite this melody **an octave higher**, using the treble clef as shown.

10

6 Add the correct rest(s) at the places marked ∗ in these two melodies to make each bar complete. [10]

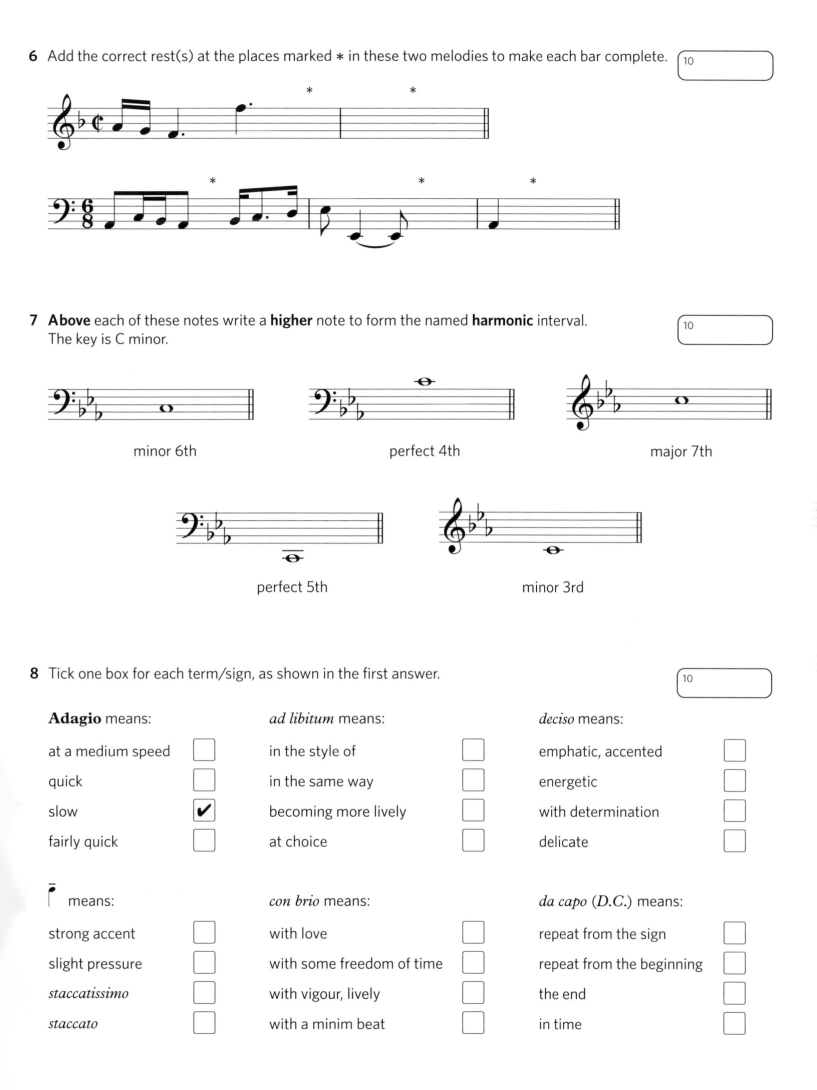

7 **Above** each of these notes write a **higher** note to form the named **harmonic** interval. The key is C minor. [10]

minor 6th   perfect 4th   major 7th

perfect 5th   minor 3rd

8 Tick one box for each term/sign, as shown in the first answer. [10]

Adagio means:		*ad libitum* means:		*deciso* means:	
at a medium speed	☐	in the style of	☐	emphatic, accented	☐
quick	☐	in the same way	☐	energetic	☐
slow	✔	becoming more lively	☐	with determination	☐
fairly quick	☐	at choice	☐	delicate	☐

˰ means:		*con brio* means:		*da capo* (*D.C.*) means:	
strong accent	☐	with love	☐	repeat from the sign	☐
slight pressure	☐	with some freedom of time	☐	repeat from the beginning	☐
staccatissimo	☐	with vigour, lively	☐	the end	☐
staccato	☐	with a minim beat	☐	in time	☐

9 Look at this melody and then answer the questions below.

Write your answer to question (b) on the stave below.

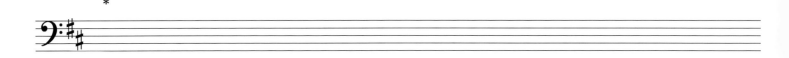

(a) (i) Answer TRUE or FALSE to these sentences:

       The melody begins on the third beat of the bar. ....

       Every **complete** bar in this melody contains
       at least one note of the tonic triad of B minor. ....

  (ii) How many times does the 7th degree
       of the scale of B minor occur in this melody? ....

 (iii) Give the letter name of the **highest** note in the melody. ....

 (iv) Complete this sentence:

       The triplet (⌐³⌐ ♩ ♩ ♩) in bar 7 means
       three crotchets (quarter notes) in the time of ....

(b) Using the blank stave above question (a), write out the melody from the beginning of bar 5
to the end of the music using notes and rests of **half the value**. Remember to put in the new
time signature at the place marked ✳, and remember to group (beam) the notes correctly.

10

Theory Paper   Grade 3   2019   C

Duration 1½ hours

Candidates should answer ALL questions.
Write your answers on this paper — no others will be accepted.
Answers must be written clearly and neatly — otherwise marks may be lost.

TOTAL MARKS
100

1   Add the missing bar-lines to each of these **three** melodies, which all begin on the first beat
of the bar.

10

2 (a) Add the correct clef and any necessary accidentals to make the scale of B♭ major.
Do **not** use a key signature.

10

   (b) Using semibreves (whole notes), write one octave of the scale of C♯ **harmonic** minor,
descending, with key signature.

3 Describe each of these melodic intervals, giving the type and number (e.g. major 3rd, perfect 4th). The keys are named, and in each case the lower note is the key note.

[10]

A minor

Type ....

Number ....

D major

Type ....

Number ....

Eb major

Type ....

Number ....

F minor

Type ....

Number ....

F# minor

Type ....

Number ....

4 Give the letter name of each of these notes. The first answer is given.

[10]

C sharp
....

....

....

....

....

....

5 Rewrite this melody with the notes correctly grouped (beamed).

[10]

6 Add the correct clef and key signature to each of these tonic triads.

10

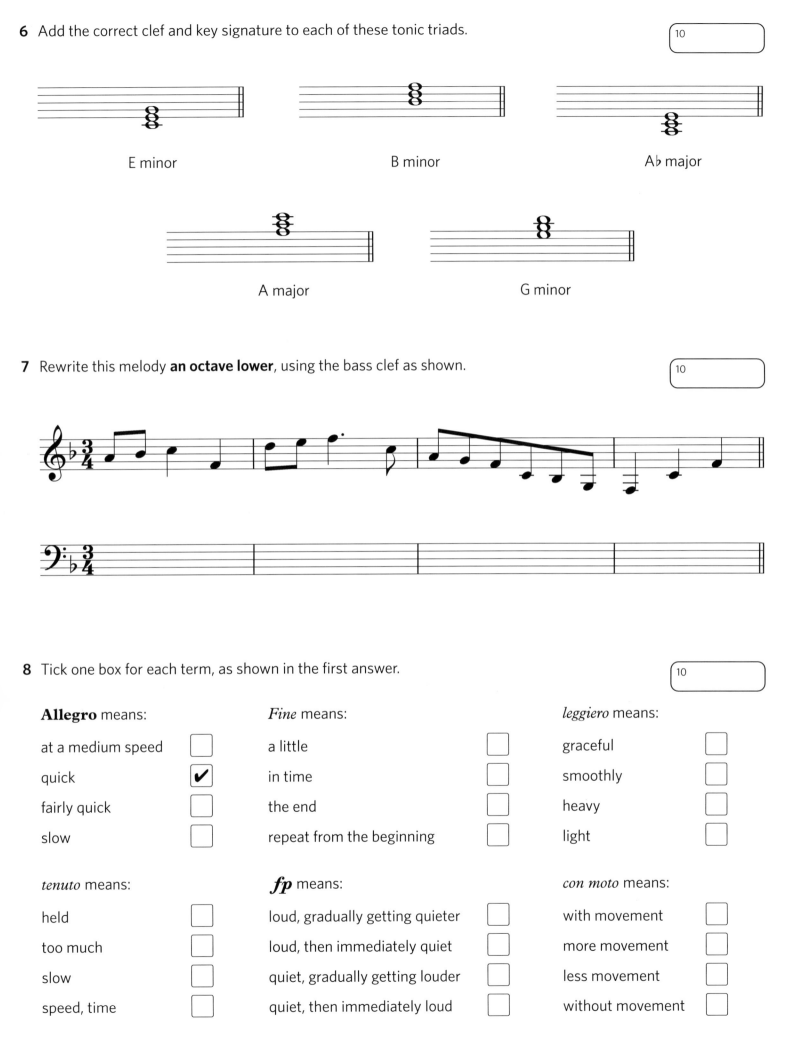

E minor

B minor

A♭ major

A major

G minor

7 Rewrite this melody **an octave lower**, using the bass clef as shown.

10

8 Tick one box for each term, as shown in the first answer.

10

Allegro means:

at a medium speed ☐
quick ✔
fairly quick ☐
slow ☐

Fine means:

a little ☐
in time ☐
the end ☐
repeat from the beginning ☐

leggiero means:

graceful ☐
smoothly ☐
heavy ☐
light ☐

tenuto means:

held ☐
too much ☐
slow ☐
speed, time ☐

fp means:

loud, gradually getting quieter ☐
loud, then immediately quiet ☐
quiet, gradually getting louder ☐
quiet, then immediately loud ☐

con moto means:

with movement ☐
more movement ☐
less movement ☐
without movement ☐

9 Look at this melody and then answer the questions below.

Write your answer to question (b) on the stave below.

(a) (i) The melody is in the key of E♭ major.
Which other key has the same key signature?   10

(ii) Answer TRUE or FALSE to this sentence:

Every **complete** bar in this melody contains
at least one note of the tonic triad of E♭ major. ....

(iii) Give the number of the bar that contains the **quietest** note in the melody. Bar ....

(iv) How many times does the rhythm 𝅘𝅥. 𝅘𝅥 occur in this melody? ....

(v) Underline one of the following words that best describes how bar 3 should be played:

legato (smoothly)   or   *staccato* (detached)

(b) Using the blank stave above question (a), write out the melody from the beginning of bar 5 to the end of the music using notes and a rest of **twice the value**. Remember to put in the new time signature at the place marked *, and remember to group (beam) the notes correctly.   10

Theory Paper   Grade 3   2019   S

Duration 1½ hours

Candidates should answer ALL questions.
Write your answers on this paper — no others will be accepted.
Answers must be written clearly and neatly — otherwise marks may be lost.

TOTAL MARKS
100

1 Add the time signature to each of these five melodies.

10

2 Add the correct rest(s) at the places marked ∗ in these two melodies to make each bar complete.

10

3 Using semibreves (whole notes), write one octave of the scales named below.

[10]

F **melodic** minor, **ascending**, without key signature but including any necessary accidentals.

E major, **descending**, with key signature.

4 Write the key signature and tonic triad of each of the following keys.

[10]

G major

Bb major

C# minor

A minor

Eb major

5 Describe each of these melodic intervals, giving the type and number (e.g. major 3rd, perfect 4th). The keys are named, and in each case the lower note is the key note.

[10]

A major

Type ....

Number ....

C minor

Type ....

Number ....

G minor

Type ....

Number ....

Ab major

Type ....

Number ....

F# minor

Type ....

Number ....

6 Rewrite this melody with the notes correctly grouped (beamed). [10]

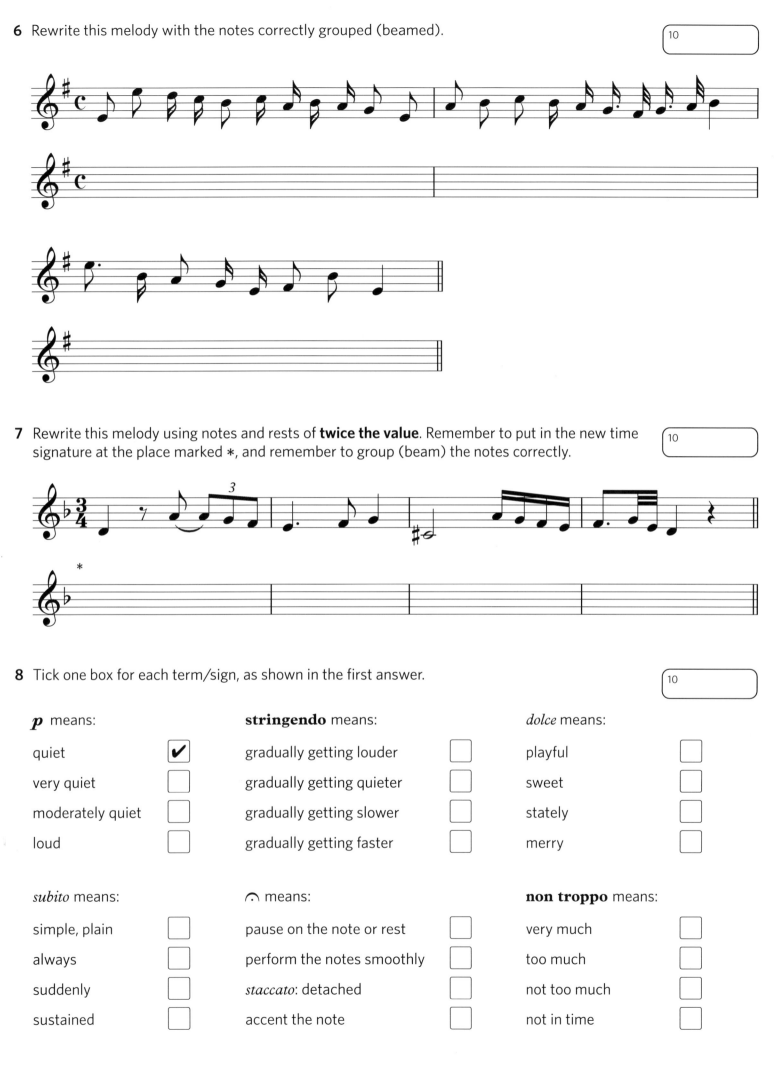

7 Rewrite this melody using notes and rests of **twice the value**. Remember to put in the new time signature at the place marked ∗, and remember to group (beam) the notes correctly. [10]

8 Tick one box for each term/sign, as shown in the first answer. [10]

p means:		**stringendo** means:		*dolce* means:	
quiet	✔	gradually getting louder	☐	playful	☐
very quiet	☐	gradually getting quieter	☐	sweet	☐
moderately quiet	☐	gradually getting slower	☐	stately	☐
loud	☐	gradually getting faster	☐	merry	☐

subito means:		⌒ means:		**non troppo** means:	
simple, plain	☐	pause on the note or rest	☐	very much	☐
always	☐	perform the notes smoothly	☐	too much	☐
suddenly	☐	*staccato*: detached	☐	not too much	☐
sustained	☐	accent the note	☐	not in time	☐

9 Look at this melody and then answer the questions below.

Write your answer to question (b) on the stave below.

(a) (i) Describe the time signature as: simple or compound   ....   [10]

duple, triple or quadruple   ....

(ii) The melody is in the key of B minor. Name the degree of
the scale (e.g. 2nd, 3rd) of the second note of bar 1 (marked *).   ....

(iii) Which other key has the same key signature as B minor?   ....

(iv) How many demisemiquavers (32nd notes)
is the second note of bar 3 (marked ↓) worth?   ....

(v) Give the numbers of two complete bars that have the same rhythm.   Bars .... and ....

(b) Using the blank stave above question (a), write out the melody from the beginning of bar 5
to the end of bar 8 **an octave higher**, using the treble clef as shown.   [10]

18

This bite-sized book  useful overview of l and will help you tc

- Understand tl
- How to achieve ... others
- Be a great team member and make a positive contribution
- Solve problems quicker by working together with others
- Embrace diversity and inclusivity in the workplace

It is the long history of humankind (and animal kind, too) that those who learned to collaborate and improvise most effectively have prevailed

Charles Darwin

Why is collaboration important?

Collaboration brings people together and helps to fuel an open environment where we can all feel valued and respected for our diversity of experience. Collaborating well with others and pulling together as a team with a common purpose can be highly motivating and helps us to feel more energised and involved.

When everyone contributes and plays to their strengths and pulls together, problems can be solved faster and new opportunities created. Collaboration also encourages a much more inclusive culture.

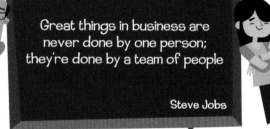

Great things in business are never done by one person; they're done by a team of people

Steve Jobs

What is collaboration?

Collaboration, essentially, is when two or more people work together towards achieving a common goal by sharing experience, skills and ideas. A key factor in the overall success of collaboration is how well we can perform together as a team.

In many ways collaboration is about cooperation and coordination and relies on a willingness to want to listen, understand and learn from each other. To collaborate well we need to be able to communicate effectively with each other.

Individually, we are one drop.
Together, we are an ocean

Ryunosuke Satoro

The benefits of collaboration

In a rapidly evolving and competitive world where innovation is key it has become increasingly important to encourage creativity and cross-fertilisation of ideas. Continual improvement relies on fresh thinking and implementing new ways of doing things.

Being able to collaborate well with others is one of the key employability skills for the future and outlined over the next few pages are some of the key benefits.

Individual commitment to a group effort - that is what makes a team work, a company work, a society work, a civilisation work

Vince Lombardi

Build high-performing teams

Working together provides a great opportunity for us to share our experience and we can learn so much from each other. Learning how to collaborate well will help us to improve our team-building skills and build a useful network to achieve better results.

Collaboration often requires input from other teams across organisations and this can provide an opportunity to boost cross-departmental relationships. An increasing amount of evidence demonstrates that new employees learn better and faster when they are placed in collaborative teams.

Solve problems

Collaborative problem-solving can offer some advantages over individual problem solving because tasks and roles can be shared. A rich diversity in a team means that the differing expertise and views can make complex problem-solving easier and faster.

When we all contribute and play to our strengths, challenges and new opportunities encourage dialogue and accelerate solutions. We can stimulate each other which will lead to enhanced creativity and more innovative solutions.

Inspire innovation

Innovation and the successful implementation of new ideas is crucial in being able to improve processes, increase efficiency, bring new and improved products and services to market, and ultimately improve results, profitability and sustainability.

In most situations it takes a team of people to implement new ideas and collaborating well together can make for a more exciting and enjoyable process. It also means that, as a team, we can celebrate the fruits of our labour knowing that we have all played our part in making innovation happen.

Connect hybrid workers

Hybrid working allows us a more flexible approach and this option of working can deliver some great benefits. It can also be quite lonely, so being able to collaborate with others through a variety of collaboration tools on a regular basis mitigates the risk of isolation and even disengagement.

To ensure collaboration equity it is important to be able to contribute and communicate with everyone in our team regardless of our location. Keeping an open dialogue and communicating regularly will help with successful collaboration.

Cultivate great relationships

Collaboration will enable us to build a strong network of supportive people who may well be able to help us through challenging times. It is important to have people in our lives who we can trust and confide in.

When we collaborate well, we will cultivate great relationships, and this can boost our overall wellbeing, confidence and sense of self-worth. Over the next few pages are some suggestions on how to collaborate well with others ...

Success is best when
it's shared

Howard Schultz

How to collaborate with others

Alone we can do so little;
together we can do so much

Helen Keller

Embrace collaboration

Sometimes we may prefer to work on our own and we may not always welcome the experience of collaborating with others. More and more in business the need to collaborate is being identified as a vital ingredient for success, so it is helpful to positively embrace collaboration.

Exploring and clearly understanding the benefits of collaboration is the first step to being a great team member.

People may not remember
exactly what you did, or what
you said, but they will always
remember how you made
them feel

Maya Angelou

Adopt a positive attitude

When we are working with other people it is important to be aware of the mindset and energy we bring to each situation. Being around people who have a positive and solution-focused attitude can have an energising effect and help us to be more productive.

Even in situations where there may be a conflict of opinions, we can still present our views in a positive way. The tone we choose to take can have a big impact on how we make other people feel.

Manage stress levels

We can be deeply affected by another person's stress levels. When we are around people who are in a highly stressed state it can create a great deal of anxiety which can lead to conflict and even arguments.

Taking personal responsibility and being aware of our own stress levels is important, especially as burnout is so prevalent in the hectic world that we live in. Looking after our personal wellbeing and taking time for self-care will help us to be better collaborators.

Be well organised

Collaboration is about coordinating well with others, so it is important to be well organised and establish working systems that can be clearly communicated to others. If we are untidy and work in chaos this will hinder the progress of projects and make things difficult for other people within the team.

Being good at planning and time management will help us to be calmer and more in control. Respecting our own time as well as other people's is very important. Being on time for meetings and well prepared is a fundamental part of great collaboration and good manners too!

When you talk,
you are only repeating
what you already know.
But if you listen,
you may learn something new

Dalai Lama

Listen to understand

Great listening skills is one of the most powerful ways to encourage constructive collaboration. When we practise active listening, we are listening with purpose and with a deep desire to want to really hear and understand what someone else is saying.

Most people will have something to say and something to contribute, so it's important that we ensure that everyone gets equal airtime. Great collaborators demonstrate that they are actively listening and avoid distractions by being present and focusing on what someone else is saying.

Appreciation can make a day
- even change a life.
Your willingness to put it into
words is all that is necessary

Margaret Cousins

Show appreciation

Taking some time to reflect on what other people are contributing and looking for opportunities to express our appreciation is a great way to motivate people. This can also encourage future collaborations.

One way to boost people's wellbeing and morale is to show them that you value and appreciate what they do, and this is about recognising hard work and achievements. Sometimes just a simple "thank you" can boost morale, strengthen teamwork and make a collaboration feel well worthwhile.

Wisdom requires a flexible mind

Dan Carlin

Be flexible

Being a great collaborator means going with the flow and being open and adaptable to changing situations and circumstances. A flexible approach allows us to expand our thinking and explore and discover a broader range of options that are potentially available to us.

Being able to think on our feet, and adjust accordingly, will help us to be responsive and agile. Actively seeking out new experiences will help us to be more flexible and encourage a growth mindset.

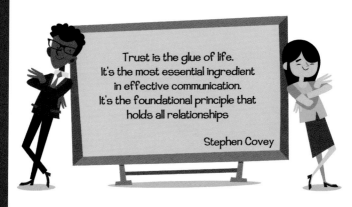

Trust is the glue of life.
It's the most essential ingredient
in effective communication.
It's the foundational principle that
holds all relationships

Stephen Covey

Foster trust

Trust is essential for any successful collaboration and people need to feel psychologically safe about sharing thoughts, ideas and suggestions. Creating and maintaining an environment that fosters trust is so necessary for collaborations to thrive.

Fostering trust can also help us to be more open and receptive to different perspectives and the more open we are with each other the more we will be able to support each other. This in turn will result in more confident collaborations.

When you need to innovate,
you need collaboration

Marissa Mayer

32

Explore collaboration tools

As we work more and more with technology there are some great collaboration tools and opportunities available. Keeping team messaging apps open for quick communication and collaboration is just one simple way to keep connected and share information and ideas.

Collaboration tools can also be of a non-technological nature such as using flip charts, Post-it notes or whiteboards in meetings. It is well worth exploring everyone's preferred method and differing approaches.

It is literally true that you can succeed best and quickest by helping others to succeed

Napoleon Hill

Help others to succeed

Great collaborators are self-sufficient when they need to be and know when they need to reach out to the team for support. Whilst a bit of healthy competition can sometimes motivate teams it is important to keep our eye on the overall goal. Focusing on win-win outcomes is key to the collective effort.

One of the greatest rewards that great collaboration delivers is the positive impact that it can have on those around us. Knowing that our collaborative input has helped others to succeed is the greatest reward of all.

If you want to go fast, go alone.
If you want to go far, go together

African proverb

Find a group of people who
challenge and inspire you,
spend a lot of time with them,
and it will change your life

Amy Poehler

COLLABORATION

How to coordinate well with each other

 BE FLEXIBLE

LISTEN TO UNDERSTAND

 HELP OTHERS TO SUCCEED

 manage YOUR STRESS

 BE WELL ORGANISED ✓

 EXPLORE COLLABORATION TOOLS

SHOW **APPRECIATION**

 ADOPT A POSITIVE ATTITUDE

FOSTER TRUST

 ENJOY COLLABORATING

Collaboration fuels a fertile playground for inspiration and innovation

Liggy Webb

Explore more at: www.liggywebb.com